Chloe and the DESERT HEROES

A Tale of Adventure in the Sonoran Desert

A Note from the Authors

Chloe and the Desert Heroes is loosely based on the original play *At Home in the Desert* by Phyllis Strupp, an Arizona Centennial Legacy Project that was performed for the public on April 30–May 1, 2014. The 38-minute play can be viewed on YouTube (see online reference 1 at the back of the book). A free teacher's kit to support classroom use of the play is also available (online reference 2).

This book is a project of the Desert Awareness Committee, whose mission is to educate people of all ages about the interdependency of the plants, animals, and people of the Sonoran Desert.

Our hope is that *Chloe and the Desert Heroes* will inspire people of all ages to respect the natural world and honor the dignity of every human being.

Enjoy the story!

The Desert Awareness Committee
www.azfcf.org/about-desert-awarcness

Authors:

Abby Hemingway
Kathleen Hindle
Brenda Olive
Phyllis Strupp
Diane Vaszily

Illustrated by Judy Speer and Georgia Taylor

Chloe and the
DESERT HEROES
A Tale of Adventure in the Sonoran Desert

The Desert Awareness Committee

The Desert Awareness Committee, Inc.
Scottsdale, Arizona

Copyright © 2017 The Desert Awareness Committee Inc.

The Desert Awareness Committee
34250 North 60th Street, Building B
Scottsdale, AZ 85266

ISBN 978-0-9746727-2-4

Library of Congress Control Number: 2016948589

All rights reserved

No part of this work may be translated, reproduced, or utilized in any form or by any means, electronic or mechanical, or in any information storage and retrieval system, or by similar or dissimilar methodology now known or hereafter developed, without the prior written permission of the publisher. The only exception to this prohibition is the reproduction of brief excerpts in connection with review or scholarly analysis.

Design and composition by Julie Bergman, Coyote House Design. The text is set in Adobe Garamond, the display in Century Gothic. The paper stock is 70 lb. Husky Offset. Printed by TUI Print & Graphic Solutions, Phoenix, Arizona.

9 8 7 6 5 4 3 2 1

In loving memory of Don Portolese,
father of Desert Awareness Committee member Brenda Olive,
whose love of the desert and generosity made this book possible

Contents

Chapter One: Trouble at School 1
Chapter Two: Lost in the Desert 3
Chapter Three: Outwitting the Predators 7
Chapter Four: The Desert Clown 11
Chapter Five: Holes in the Ground 15
Chapter Six: Dinnertime in the Desert 19
Chapter Seven: Lots of New Friends 23

Resources

Activities 27
Online References 33
Places to Visit the Sonoran Desert 34
Activity Answer Key 35

Chapter One

Trouble at School

Oh, hello! Nice to meet you. My name is Chloe. I am 12 years old. My home here in the Valley of the Sun is surrounded by the most beautiful desert in the world, also known as the Sonoran Desert.

When we first moved here, I hated this prickly, scraggly, dried-up desert. Then one day I got lost, and the heroes of the desert helped me find my way home. Now I feel right at home in the Sonoran Desert, knowing it is full of such wonderful neighbors.

What's that? You don't know about the heroes of the Sonoran Desert? Well then, just in case you ever get lost and need a helping hand, let me share the story of my adventures with the desert heroes.

Mom and I used to live way down in the city with Peppy, our black Labrador retriever. We had a cozy home. I went to a school nearby, and had a great group of friends in my neighborhood. Oh, what fun we used to have together!

Then something really bad happened. One spring day Mom and I came home after school, and there was a big "Foreclosed" sign on our house. We had to move right then and there. I cried and cried and cried over leaving my friends and home behind, but at least my dog Peppy got to come with us.

Fortunately, my Aunt Ruth let us move into her big house up north, right in the desert. But I missed my old friends so much it hurt. At my new school, it was hard to make friends in the middle of the school year. Since I was new and alone, the bullies wouldn't stop pestering me. One day, a bully said I was so ugly that it was illegal, and that I should leave Arizona because I didn't belong here. It was horrible!

I was so angry when I got home. Mom was working, so Aunt Ruth tried to comfort me, but nothing helped, not even chocolate chip cookies and milk. I told her I hated living here, and I wanted to move back to my old home and be with my true friends.

Then Aunt Ruth suggested I take Peppy out for a walk in the desert to get some fresh spring air and sunshine. She warned me to put Peppy on a leash and avoid the path to the north. I said OK—but I ignored her advice on both counts. That was a *b-i-i-i-g* mistake! Peppy and I were out walking on the trail to the north, when suddenly a rabbit hopped by. Peppy took off after the rabbit! I ran after Peppy and called her, but she was gone. And I was lost.

Then I heard coyotes howling in the distance. Oh no, I thought, they sound hungry. They must be after Peppy—and maybe even me.

I was so scared I didn't know what to do. Then I started screaming, "Help! Help!" even though I knew no one could hear me.

Chapter Two

Lost in the Desert

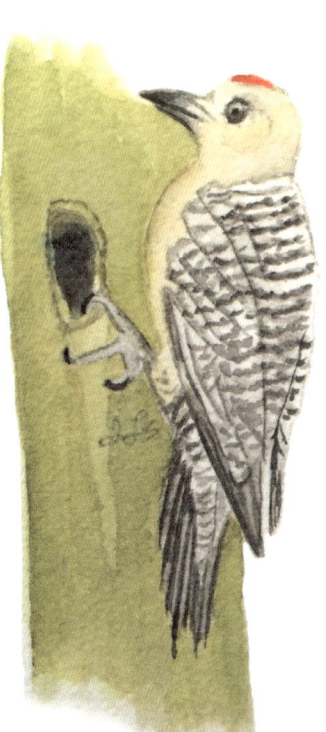

Suddenly I heard a very strange sound, almost like gunfire: uh-uh-uh-uh, uh-uh-uh-uh. I looked around, and at the top of a small saguaro just 6 feet away was a handsome striped bird with a big red spot on his head.

"What are you doing here?" I cried out.

"What do you mean, what am I doing here? This is *my* home, and you are in *my* territory. What are *you* doing here?"

"My name is Chloe, and I was out for a walk with my dog Peppy, but Peppy ran off after a rabbit and I got lost trying to find her. Now I can't find my way home."

"Oh, nice to meet you, Chloe. My name is *Melanerpes uropygialis,*" the bird said.

"Mel what? What kind of name is that?" I asked.

"That's my scientific name. But you can just call me Mel."

"OK, Mel, nice to meet you. But I thought parrots were the only talking birds. How on earth did you learn to talk?"

"How did *you* learn to talk?"

"From my family."

"Me too."

Looking around, I wondered out loud, "Mel, how can you possibly live out here in the desert? I don't see anything that looks like a comfortable home."

Pointing with his long beak, he said, "OK, see that saguaro over there? The one that is 40 feet tall with a dozen arms?"

"You mean the one with all the holes?"

"Exactly! Guess who pecked out those holes?"

"Who?"

"Me, all by myself," Mel squeaked with pride.

"Well, it couldn't have been that hard. Isn't the saguaro full of water and squishy inside?"

"Go ahead, Chloe, go over there and touch the skin—but watch out for the spines."

Did you know?

- Sharp spikes on the tip of its tail anchor a Gila woodpecker as it pecks a hole.
- Gila woodpeckers dig out a nest hole called a "boot" in a saguaro.
- A nest inside a saguaro is 30 degrees cooler than the outside.
- Gila woodpeckers bang loudly on metal objects to attract a mate.
- Gila woodpeckers keep saguaros healthy by eating damaged tissue.

Saguaro "Boot"

I walked over to the saguaro and pushed it with my finger. "Yikes, it's tough as nails! How on earth did you peck holes in it, Mel?"

"See this sturdy beak of mine? And my thick neck? We Gila woodpeckers are natives of the Sonoran Desert, just like the saguaro. The saguaro can live up to 200 years, growing up to 50 feet tall and weighing 2,000 pounds."

"Mel, you know so much about the saguaro, you sound like a plant expert—a botanist!"

Beaming with pride, Mel continued, "We're one of the few birds that can peck a hole in the saguaro to make a nest that keeps us warm in winter and cool in summer. Our babies are safe way up there, too."

"Oh, how I wish Peppy and I were safe at home."

"Look Chloe, I don't know where you live, but I do know my way around this desert pretty well. Would you like some help in finding your way home?"

"Yes, Mel, that would be wonderful! I feel better already, knowing you'll be my guide."

"OK, let's get started. Which direction did you come from?"

"Uhhhh … I'm not sure."

"OK, which way do you want to go?"

"Ummmm … I have no clue."

"Do you remember any landmarks you saw along the way?"

"No. Mel, this is a hopeless situation; you're wasting your time trying to help me. And … I'm kind of glad to be lost anyway."

"Why?"

"Because I don't have any friends and the bullies at school pick on me every day."

"Oh, is that all? The Sonoran Desert is full of heroes that can help you."

"Really? What kind of heroes could possibly live in this prickly, scraggly, dried-up desert?"

"The desert is full of heroes, Chloe. The plants and the animals of the desert are survival heroes: they have great courage and can handle just about any challenge that comes along, even getting lost. Why, yes indeedy, here's a desert hero right now: Hoardy, the packrat!"

Chapter Three

Outwitting the Predators

"Hi there! Good to see you, Mel," Hoardy mumbled though a piece of teddy bear cholla in his mouth.

"Hoardy, I'd like you to meet my friend Chloe, who is trying to find her way home," said Mel.

"Hi Hoardy, nice to meet you! Is this where you live?"

"Hello, Chloe! Yes, this is my midden, my home. I would invite you in, but I purposely put teddy bear cholla, with all those nasty barbs at the ends of their spines, around the entrance, to discourage my enemies from following me inside."

"Your enemies? But you seem so nice. Why do you have enemies?"

"It has nothing to do with being nice, Chloe. You're nice, and yet bullies pick on you."

"How on earth did you know about my problems with bullies?"

"Oh, let's just say a little birdie told me," said Hoardy, as he winked at Mel. "Anyway, my enemies are predators—you know, animals that eat other animals."

"Yes, now I remember, we studied the Food Web—what eats what—in school."

Hoardy stood up on his hind legs and chewed a seed as he declared, "Owls, bobcats, coyotes, and even roadrunners would all love to take a bite out of me."

"That sounds even worse than getting teased."

"Well, I don't take it personally. They're hungry, and I taste good to them. That's all there is to it."

"Aren't you afraid of living here, with predators all around that want to eat you?"

"Nope," Hoardy answered. "The best way for a little fella like me to survive in this dangerous place is to run strong and outwit my predators, rather than fear them. In the desert, you can run scared or run strong, but you can't do both."

"Hey Hoardy, getting back to your midden, couldn't I just have a little peak inside, somehow?" I asked.

"Well, OK. To tell you the truth, I kind of like to show it off. I let my friends have their fun teasing me by calling me 'Hoardy' and all. But actually, I am quite unlike my other packrat buddies, who pick up anything they can get their little claws into. I'm not being critical—they do a lot to keep our environment clear of debris—but I am very discerning about what I decorate my midden with. And yes, I did say 'decorate.'"

Seeing the surprised look on my face, Mel confirmed, "Yes indeedy, Hoardy is a debris artist."

"Really? What kind of debris do you like the most?" I inquired.

"I have always been a fan of Native American culture, and lucky for me, some of the people in houses near here collect Navajo art."

"Oh, please let me see!" I begged.

"OK, I'll just take away some of this cholla. You're going to love this! My pride and joy is this modern-day replica of a sand painting featuring the sun, known as Tawa to the Navajo."

"Where did you get this beautiful painting?" I asked, gazing at the strange figure.

"Tawa"

"Oh, some people who live nearby left it on their back patio one night."

Looking around, I said, "Hoardy, you have done a wonderful job decorating this midden. You must be so happy here!"

Hoardy thought for a moment. "Happy? Well sort of, but I wish I could get more information about sand painting: how it is done and why it is done. I can never go to school, like you can, to find out more about it … so it makes me a little sad."

"Oh, goody," I squealed, "now I have something to share with you! When I was in fourth grade, we learned many things about the Sonoran Desert in school. But I particularly remember the story about sand painting. The sand painter, "Hatałii" in Navajo, paints meaningful symbols on the ground during a healing ceremony. The person who is ill sits in the middle of the painting to absorb the healing energies of the spirits."

"Wow, imagine that!" said Hoardy, with wide eyes.

"This is all very interesting, but we have to get Chloe home before sundown, for heaven's sake," interjected Mel.

"Rats (no pun intended)!" yelled Hoardy. "Just when I am finally able to learn some important stuff about sand painting, it's time to go!"

"People who study different cultures in today's world are called cultural anthropologists. Hoardy, if you could go to school one day, I'll bet you would study cultural anthropology," I said.

"Whoa," said Hoardy. "Imagine that: me, a cultural anthropologist!"

"Listen, guys, I am not kidding," prodded Mel. "We've got to go! Hoardy, any chance you could point us in the right direction?"

Did you know?

- Packrat middens have several entries and exits, with tunnels linking storage and sleeping areas.
- Packrat middens are built, abandoned, and re-occupied over centuries.
- Packrat nests can be up to 4 feet high and 8 feet wide, inhabited by one packrat at a time.
- Packrats depend on succulent plants for water, as their bodies store very little water.

Chapter Four

The Desert Clown

Before Hoardy could answer, a rather large bird with a snake hanging from its mouth sped across the desert, parading back and forth in front of me as if to show off its prize.

"Mel, what kind of bird is this?" I asked.

"Oh, that's another desert hero: Zip the Roadrunner. He would rather run than fly. We call him the 'desert clown.'"

Zip ran off under a bush and then quickly reappeared: "Hello, Mel. Who's your friend?"

Mel pointed to me with his beak and answered, "This is Chloe, and she is wondering what you're doing."

Zip explained: "I caught a long-nosed snake for dinner. I've got to be quicker than the rattlesnake and the Harris's hawk to get a meal around here! Lizards and cactus wrens make a good meal too, but the missus preferred a small snake today."

"Zip, is there anything you don't eat?" I asked.

"Not really. I'm what you call an omnivore. Plants, animals, insects—you name it, I can eat it."

Then Mel said, "Zip, you get around, help us out. Chloe is trying to find her dog Peppy, a black lab. Have you seen her?"

"OK, Chloe, where did you last see Peppy?"

"My poor old Peppy went off chasing a rabbit when we were on the trail to the north."

"Well, I haven't seen Peppy, but I'll help you look for her. Come over this way," Zip suggested.

"Oh, look at the cute bunnies over there, jumping around each other," I giggled.

Zip and Mel laughed along with me as Zip explained, "It is mating season for the desert cottontail rabbit, Chloe. In a month or so that mama bunny will make an underground nest for her babies, insulated from the heat and safe from coyotes, hawks, and other predators."

As we continued to meander through the desert looking for Peppy, a large bird swooped down overhead. "What was that?" I screamed.

Zip replied, "That was the great horned owl on the hunt for dinner. He must have seen the rabbits, or maybe a packrat nearby."

"You mean the owl was after those cute bunny rabbits or my friend Hoardy?" I shouted.

"Yes," responded Zip. "It is the desert's natural Food Web of predator and prey in action, Chloe. The night creatures are beginning to make their appearances—listen carefully."

"I hear munching, chomping, grunting noises," I whispered.

"Oh yes, over there by the prickly pear cactus," Zip said. "Do you see? Those critters are javelina, the smallest hoofed mammals in the Sonoran Desert. They are vegetarians, neither prey nor predator. That is, except for their babies, which get eaten quite often, so they are helicopter parents for sure. The family travels together, and they have a keen sense of smell, but they sometimes bump into things because they can't see very well."

Suddenly, a blood-curdling chorus of howls rang out in the desert. "Oh no, coyotes! Did they get Peppy?" I cried to Zip and Mel.

"I don't know, but I think that's my cue. I've got to run and get dinner on the table back home. Goodbye, Chloe, and good luck finding Peppy. See you around, Mel!" And with that, Zip rushed off.

After we said goodbye, I turned to Mel: "Zip knows a lot about desert wildlife and their ways."

"Yes indeedy, we call him Zip the Zoologist, because he understands how the Food Web keeps the Circle of Life going round and round here in the Sonoran Desert. But come on—we need to find the path that leads home quickly, before it gets dark."

Did you know?

- A herd of javelina share a strong smell by rubbing scent glands on their backs against one another.
- Despite their squat shape, javelina can leap 6 feet and run up to 35 miles per hour when chased.
- Javelinas' favorite food is prickly pear cactus; their mouths cannot feel the spines.

Chapter Five

Holes in the Ground

As I looked around for the path, I noticed something strange on the ground. "Mel, look at all the holes everywhere! All different sizes. Who is making these holes? Wow, look at that one … it looks like a cave, surrounded by rocks. Should I be afraid of who lives there?"

"No, not at all. That belongs to Tory the tortoise. Here she is now. Hi, Tory!"

"Oh, good evening.… I'm on my way out to grab a bite to eat.… Have you seen any juicy flowers or grasses on your walk? I need to get a few bites before I go back in for the night. It's tough living in this hot—and cold—desert. I spend most of my time waiting in my cave until it is the perfect time to come out."

"Do you stay inside that burrow all day? And all night?" I asked.

"When it's too hot or too cold, I seek shelter in my burrow here among the rocks laid down by ancient civilizations. My great granddad told me about the people of long ago. In archaic times, the Hohokam built their homes with rocks, and now I live among the ruins. It works very well, because the rocks keep my home cool in summer and warm in winter, just as they did for the Hohokam."

"Archaic times? Like what an archaeologist studies? I never made that connection before."

"Yes, Chloe, long ago in days of old, that's what I mean. I'm kind of archaic myself, you know."

"Really, Tory? How old are you?"

"Oh, I'm almost 80 years old—but feeling quite young at heart."

"Staying alive for 80 years out here in the hot and cold desert … amazing! How do you do it, Tory?"

"I never leave my toasty burrow from November to March. When spring comes, I wander around and eat my favorite plants. Things are very tasty out here in the desert … for a hungry tortoise like me! It's a good thing I eat so much, so there's less kindling on the desert floor when the next wildfire comes along."

"So you are a desert hero, too, Tory. Do you have any friends?"

"Oh yes, some of us tortoises get together every once in a while. After a warm rain we all come out and play in the puddles. Gives me a chance to take a bit of a soak and a nice long drink. I don't get a chance to drink very much out here. My days are spent wandering, napping, and thinking. Not too much gets in my way. Life is good in the Sonoran Desert. We all seem to live well together.… Now, if you will excuse me, I'll be on my way."

Did you know?

- The desert tortoise can go without food or water for over a year, relying on water stored in its bladder.
- The desert tortoise spends 95% of its life in a small burrow to avoid extreme hot and cold temperatures.
- A desert tortoise that survives to age 20 is likely to live until age 80.

"Sure, Tory. But before you go, can you tell me who makes all these little holes I see all over the desert floor?" I asked.

"Most of the holes are made by little packrats and mice, but that shiny one over there with the soft-looking welcome mat was made by my friend Tara, the tarantula."

"Eeeek! A tarantula! How scary! Where is it?"

"Just look under a bush; you will soon see her running across the bare ground toward her home. I doubt if she will bother you, though."

"Oh my. I don't think I want to see her at all. I'd better be getting home myself."

"Well, I never have a problem with her. She is a lot like me: stays in her burrow unless she gets hungry. She almost never hunts during the day, just at night."

"What does she eat?"

"I have seen her jump on a lizard or catch crawling insects. She seems to have a way of drinking the juices out of them and leaving the carcass behind. I always wondered about that clever trick myself."

"I learned in school that they have fangs."

"Gosh. That must be how she sucks the juices out of her prey!"

"And tarantulas have eight eyes, too."

"Imagine that, eight eyes! No wonder she can see things above, below, and all around her. Maybe I'll sit and watch her more closely some day. But I can never take my mind off food for very long—like now! I'm off to the wildflower patch for a quick bite before bedtime. Goodbye."

After we said goodbye, I whispered to Mel, "Do you see any tarantulas? I still don't know if I want to meet one. They really scare me."

Gazing at me kindly, Mel said, "You need to be at the right place at the right time, when the sun is very low in the sky. Tarantulas either sit very still, or run from bush to bush to stay out of sight. They could care less about you. But you might be able to see one if you find her burrow. They are always lined with silk to make it soft for them."

"You mean they spin webs?"

"They don't spin webs, but the mama tarantula makes silk and uses it at the entrance to her burrow. This silk catches sand and dirt—like the welcome mat at your front door."

"But how in the world does she make a burrow?" I asked. "She has nothing to use for digging."

"She uses her fangs and legs like I would use my beak. It's easy for her to shovel little rocks around. She moves them around one at a time, just like a geologist would explore one rock at a time."

"Fascinating—a geologist with fangs and eight eyes! I like examining rocks. Maybe I'll become a geologist one day," I mused.

"Just one more reason why we need to get you home safely right now. We must find a desert hero who knows where the path is. And I know who can help us!"

Did you know?

- After mating, a female tarantula will consume the male if he doesn't get away quickly.
- Female tarantulas can live up to 30 years, while males live about 10 years
- Tarantulas depend on ground vibrations to detect and ambush prey.
- Tarantulas have retractable claws, like cats, to grasp when climbing.
- When molting, a tarantula can grow a new leg to replace a damaged one.

Chapter Six

Dinnertime in the Desert

"Oh Campy, we need you! Where are you?" Mel called out.

"Char-char-char-char-char!" someone answered back.

"Mel, what's that rackety sound?" I asked.

Mel landed on a saguaro arm. Pointing with his long beak, he said, "Look over there, Chloe! That's Campy. She's a cactus wren—Arizona's state bird, formally known as Campylorhynchus brunneicapillus. Hey Campy, over here!"

A busy little bird hopped over to us, wings puffed out.

"What's up, Mel?" she buzzed.

"Meet my friend Chloe. She's lost and I knew you would be able to help her find her way home, given how serious you are about nesting."

"Hello, Chloe. Hmmm. I'll do what I can, but this is not a good time: we're having dinner!"

She scurried off to a clump of teddy bear cholla cactus nearby, where three fledglings were exploring the desert floor.

"Tek-tek-tek-tek-tek-tek," Campy said to her little ones, poking around the rubble on the ground.

"Mel, what's she saying to them?"

"She's explaining that their bills are the perfect tool for getting under stones and dried leaves and seeing what's underneath. Oh look, Campy got a yummy treat!"

Mel and I watched Campy pass a wasp on to the young wrens. They promptly fell into a loud squabble over it, with one of them gobbling it down and the other two attacking the lucky wren.

Campy's throaty voice increased to a rapid-fire pitch as she scolded, "Kids, you won't get food into your stomach by bullying each other! Now get busy. No, no, no, no, no! Don't try to move those big rocks! There's plenty to eat under the smaller pebbles and leaf litter."

"Char-char-char-char-char!" called another nearby cactus wren.

"That's their father," Campy explained. "He's busy finishing another nest for our next brood. I'll be able to begin lining it with feathers soon."

"Oh my, you are busy, Campy." I looked around and saw several nests tucked snugly into the chain fruit cholla plants around us. "But why not save some time and use one of these existing nests?"

"Oh no, no, no, no, no!" she buzzed. "We always make a new nest for each clutch of eggs. And I get to decide where. We even build extra nests. Some we will use for roosting at night. Some are there just to confuse our predators!"

As I looked around at the thick stand of chain fruit cholla plants, there was something familiar about the place, but I didn't quite know why.

"Char-char-char-char-char!" Campy's male partner for life fluttered in and surveyed the scene. Satisfied that Mel and I were harmless observers, he flitted down near his raucous fledglings and joined the search for insects.

"Oooooh! A grasshopper!" said Campy. "The juicy ones are the best! We usually don't have to look for water because we get enough from the insects we eat."

The little wrens circled in on the insect, trying to crack the grasshopper's hard outer covering with their beaks. Pappa wren moved in and showed them how to get the job done. Mel and I watched the grasshopper disappear.

"Do you eat anything other than insects?" I asked Campy.

"Mostly insects. Beetles, wasps, grasshoppers, ants, spiders, moths and butterflies, and such would take over the desert if it weren't for us. Sometimes we even get small lizards and frogs. But we also eat some seeds. The seeds of the saguaro fruits are a special treat. We will introduce our kids to them this summer!"

"Campy knows so much about insects," I said to Mel. "She is like a scientist who studies insects—the entomologist."

"You might not know it, but Campy and the cactus wrens are true heroes of the desert," Mel told me. "Although they eat mainly insects, they spread tiny black saguaro seeds

Did you know?

- The cactus wren is the state bird of Arizona.
- A cactus wren pair can impale a squirrel on a cholla spine to protect their young.

around the desert, through their droppings. It means baby saguaros have a chance to take root and grow in a whole lot of new places."

Suddenly, a thought popped into my head. "Wait a minute! I passed by this chain fruit cholla thicket when I first left the trail to look for Peppy! Campy, do you know where the trail to the south is?"

"Of course, of course! Go around that jojoba, then past the big saguaro. You will see the trail from there. Good luck, Chloe! Hey, kids! How many times must I tell you—stop fighting!"

Mel flew ahead and called to me so I could find the trail. Then I saw Black Mountain to the south, and the sun setting in the west … and I knew I was headed in the right direction, toward home.

So I began to run up the trail, with Mel flying along with me from saguaro to saguaro. Once again I heard coyotes howling in the distance. I asked Mel if he thought the coyotes had gotten my Peppy.

"Why don't you call her?" Mel suggested.

Did you know?

- Coyotes howl, yelp, huff, bark, and wail to keep track of family members.
- Coyotes walk lightly on their toes to sneak up on prey.
- Coyotes hunt cooperatively: one distracts the prey while another pounces.
- Coyotes can run up to 40 miles per hour.

Chapter Seven

Lots of New Friends

As I approached the dirt road that goes by our house, I yelled at the top of my lungs, "Peppy! Peppy!" Then I heard a familiar bark. In the distance, I saw Mom and Aunt Ruth standing in the driveway—with Peppy by their side on a leash, wagging her tail a mile a minute.

Tears of joy filled my eyes. Then I looked around to say thank you to Mel, but he was gone. My hero Mel had slipped away without a peep. So I yelled out into the desert, "Thank you Mel! Goodbye! You have taught me how to be at home in the desert. I will remember you every time I see a hole in a saguaro!"

In the distance I heard "Awk awk awk, awk awk awk!" I knew it was Mel saying goodbye.

I was so happy to be home! I told Mom and Aunt Ruth all about my adventures with Mel and the other desert heroes. And I told Peppy I would never ever risk her life again by not using a leash on our walks.

That night, I dreamed about my new friends Mel, Hoardy, Zip, Tory, and Campy, and all the amazing sights I had seen.

The next day, as I arrived at my school, I began to think about the bullies, and my stomach felt tied up in knots once again. Then I said to myself, "Chloe, you need to be like the desert heroes. Run strong, not scared, and outwit the bullies." I counted myself lucky that I just had bullies rather than predators to cope with. Then suddenly, I felt fearless—more confident—way down deep inside.

Later on that day, sure enough, the bullies gave me a chance to test my inner strength. They started picking on me as usual. I felt nervous, and got a lump in my throat. Then I thought to myself: if Hoardy can hang tough out in the desert, I can handle these bullies. All at once I regained my confidence and heard myself saying to the bullies: "I belong here as much as anyone else. And until a Gila woodpecker or a cactus wren throws me out, I'm staying put, no matter what you say."

The bullies started to laugh and mock me. Oh no, what am I going to do now, I wondered. Then Beth, a popular girl, stood next to me and told the bullies to buzz off and leave me alone—and they did! I said thank you to Beth, and she said she admired my courage. Then she asked me to hang out with her group of friends.

From then on, I had lots of new friends, both at school and in the desert. Thank goodness we moved in with Aunt Ruth, because now I feel right at home here in the desert. And some day, I'm going to become a botanist, so I can help preserve the saguaro and make sure Mel and his family have a home in the Sonoran Desert for many generations to come.

The End

Activities

1. Word Search

```
R G L T U J L S V S H E A Q I
L A E I P X U C C Y D A L C H
F R E X Y T J I H R C F L M L
Z K Q P C D E S E R T O O D C
W T C A Y N P V K H D O H S T
J S C G C L O W U X C D C A D
R I F E L L K S T G N W X G A
U G O S A I T C K I H E G U G
J O X P Y P Z G I E B B F A P
F L T A R K C A P R L B K R E
L O Y S Z D T Y R R P E A O F
H E B B S W K D I D Q J T R M
W G M O B B R D F H D J Z O B
W K O G K M F Y Z E Z G M Z N
P R E D A T O R S H P T B F H
```

See if you can find these 14 words:

geologist   cactus   desert
saguaro   science   predators
rabbit   prickly pear   lizard
cholla   palo verde   packrat
food web   skeleton

27

2. Word Scrambles

Unscramble the letters to find the words below:

zoologist   Sonoran Desert   sand painting   rattlesnake
predators   prickly pear   roadrunner

TETSNAAKERL _____

DSSEERTNNOOAR _____

PPRRICKEALY _____

GLOOOZIST _____

RRNNOARDUE _____

AATINGSPNNDI _____

SORREAPDT _____

3. Fill in the Blanks

Choose from the following key words to fill in the blanks:

>
> tarantula   great horned owl   coyote   tortoise
> roadrunner   Gila woodpecker   javelina   cactus wren

1. A _ _ _ _ _ _ can run 40 miles per hour.
2. The "boot" that _ _ _ _ _ _ _ _ _ _ _ _ _ _ s dig out of a saguaro, for their nest, is 30 degrees cooler inside than the outside temperature.
3. The _ _ _ _ _ _ _ _ _ _ is the state bird of Arizona.
4. The desert _ _ _ _ _ _ _ _ digs a burrow, averaging 3 to 6 feet deep, and spends 95% of its time there.
5. A _ _ _ _ _ _ _ _ _ can range in size from as small as a fingernail to as large as a dinner plate.
6. When hunting a snake, the _ _ _ _ _ _ _ _ _ _ will grab its tail and whip it around and around, hitting the snake on the ground until it is dead.
7. _ _ _ _ _ _ _ _ _ _ _ _ _ _ s have large ears that are covered with special feathers that amplify sound.
8. The _ _ _ _ _ _ _ _'s favorite food is prickly pear cactus.

4. Drawing

Draw pictures of these items you find in the Sonoran Desert.

Saguaro	Tortoise
Palo verde tree	Prickly pear cactus
Rattlesnake	Sun (Tawa)
Coyote	Ancient Indian Dwelling

5. How Well Do You Know Desert Plants?

Select the correct answer to the questions below using the following words:

palo verde   teddy bear cholla   ocotillo   saguaro
catclaw   chain fruit cholla   ironwood

1. What is the Sonoran Desert's signature plant?

2. Name the Arizona state tree.

3. Which cholla has the best defense system for bird and packrat nests?

4. What cholla cactus sister has fruit hanging from its branches?

5. Name the tree with gray bark that is strong as steel.

6. Which native bush has thorns in the shape of a feline claw?

7. Name the bush with many stems and little "lantern-like" red blossoms in the spring.

6. Food Web

Complete the food chain below by drawing a line from the predator in the middle column to the food it eats in the left column. Next, draw a line from the predators to the animal or insect in the right column who eats the predator. *Hint: There can be multiple answers for some predators.*

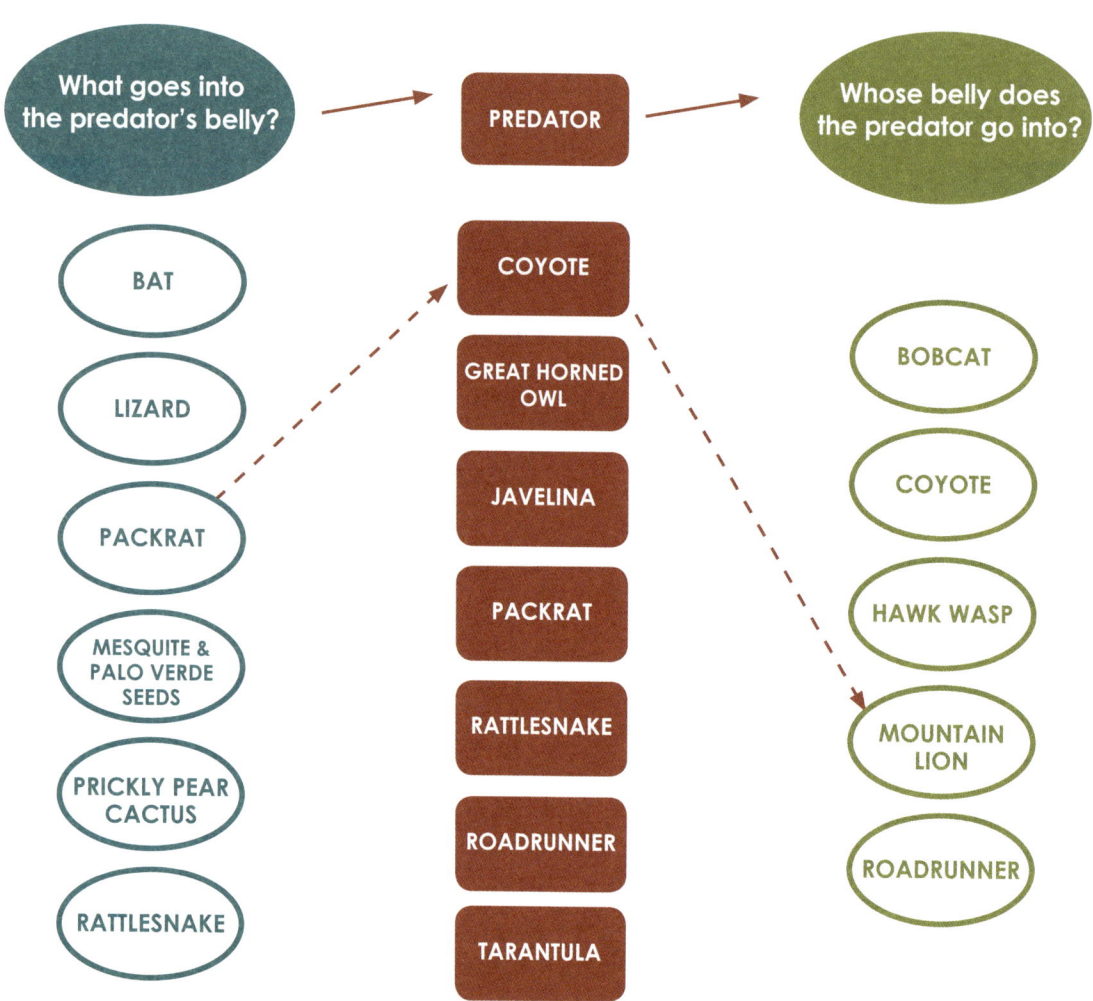

Online References

1. "At Home in the Desert" Arizona Centennial Legacy Project
   https://www.youtube.com/watch?v=UlUOihAuhls

2. "At Home in the Desert" teacher's kit for classroom use
   http://www.azfcf.org/#!about-desert-awareness/cks4

3. Desert Awareness Committee information and programs
   http://www.azfcf.org/about-desert-awareness

4. Desert animal and plant facts
   https://www.desertmuseum.org/kids/oz/long-fact-sheets/

5. Sand painting:
   navajopeople.org
   nativeamerican-art.com
   warpaths2peacepipes.com

6. Article about an Arizona elementary school project
   0http://education.nationalgeographic.org/news/cultivating-life-sonoran-desert/

Places to Visit the Sonoran Desert

Arizona-Sonora Desert Museum
desertmuseum.org

Boyce-Thompson Arboretum
ag.arizona.edu/bta

Cave Creek Regional Park
maricopacountyparks.net

Deer Valley Petroglyph Preserve
shesc.asu.edu/dvpp

Desert Awareness Park
azfcf.org/#!desert-awareness-park/cqhe

Desert Botanical Garden
dbg.org

McDowell-Sonoran Preserve
mcdowellsonoran.org

Phoenix Mountains Preserve
phoenix.gov/parks/trails

Pinnacle Peak Park
scottsdaleaz.gov/parks/pinnacle-peak-park

Saguaro National Park
nps.gov/sagu/index.htm

Spur Cross Ranch Conservation Area
maricopacountyparks.net

Activity Answer Key

1. Word Search, p. 27

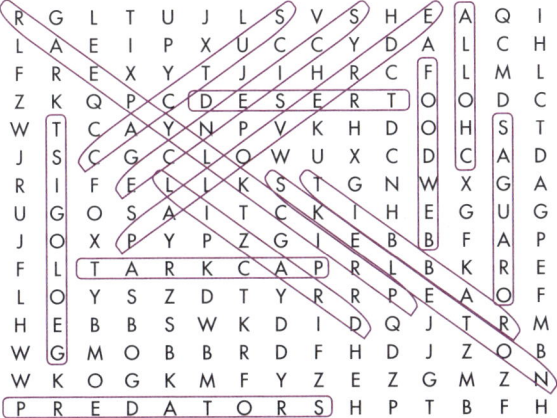

2. Word Scrambles, p. 28

rattlesnake
Sonoran Desert
prickly pear
zoologist
roadrunner
sand painting
predators

3. Fill in the Blanks, p. 29

1. coyote
2. Gila woodpecker
3. cactus wren
4. tortoise
5. tarantula
6. roadrunner
7. great horned owl
8. javelina

5. Desert Plants, p. 31

1. saguaro
2. palo verde
3. teddy bear cholla
4. chain fruit cholla
5. ironwood
6. catclaw
7. ocotillo

6. Food Web, p. 32

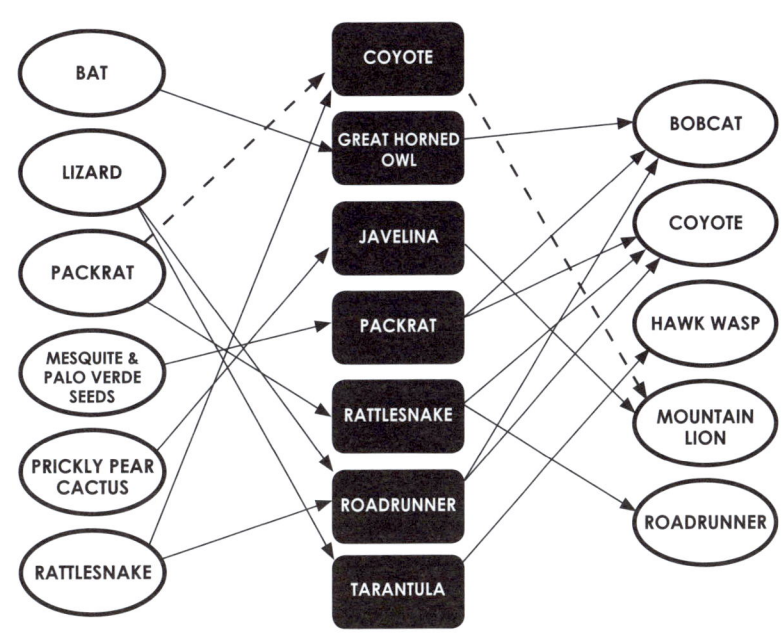